Think. Plan.

The Complete Business Planning Guide for First-Time Entrepreneurs

Table of Contents

Chapter 1: Business Startup Overview..2
Vision & Goals..2
Clarifying the Business Idea and Long-Term Vision...3
Identifying Key Goals and Objectives for Succes...10

Chapter 2: Market Research & Competitive Analysis............................16
Analyzing Industry Trends and Market Demand..19

Chapter 3: Business Structure & Legal Setup...25
Determining the Appropriate Business Entity..27
Factors to Consider When Choosing a Business Entity.....................................28
Necessary Permits, Licenses, and Compliance Requirements................................33

Chapter 4: Financial Planning & Budgeting..36
Creating a Startup Budget and Financial Projections.....................................37
Operating Expenses...45
Emergency Fund..53
Break Even Analysis...60
Financial Projections-Revenue Forecast...68
Expense Estimates...71

Cash Flow Projection..,74

Profitability Analysis..77

Exploring Funding Options (Loans, Investors, Grants) 80

Chapter 5: Branding & Marketing..84

Developing Brand Identity..85

Outlining Marketing Channels (Social Media, Website, Advertising) 87

Chapter 6: Operational Planning & Logistics..91

Strategic Objectives..91

Process Optimization..94

Resource Management..101

Risk Management...108

Logistics – Supply Chain Coordination...116

Transportation & Delivery...124

Technology Integration..132

Customer Fulfillment..140

Establishing Workflows, Suppliers, and Technological Needs.......................148

Hiring Needs and Employee Management Strategies......................................151

Chapter 7: Launch Plans & Next Steps..154

Setting Realistic Timelines for Launching..155

Creating Action Steps for the first Few Months of Business Operation.........157

Chapter 8: Examples 160

Business Idea 160

Market Research and Competitive Analysis 161

Business Structure & Legal Setup 162

Financial Planning & Budgeting 163

Branding & Marketing Strategy 165

Operational Planning & Logistics 167

Launch Plan & Next Steps 168

Think.
Plan.
Launch.

The Complete Business Planning Guide for First-Time Entrepreneurs

If you've ever said, "I want to start a business, but I don't know where to begin," this book was written for you.

There's a lot of advice out there for entrepreneurs – some of it inspiring, some of it overwhelming. It mostly lacks structure. That's what this guide gives you: a clear, step-by-step path from raw ideas to actual launch.

This is not a book about theory. It's a book about doing. Each section breaks down a part of the process – thinking through your idea, planning your strategy, and launching with purpose. You don't need a fancy degree or years of experience. You just need a plan.

Whether you're starting small or dreaming big, what matters most is that you start smart. And with this guide in hand, you will.

Let's get to work.

Chapter 1
Business Startup Overview

Vision & Goals

The process of establishing clear long-term direction and actionable steps for a business or project. A **vision** describes the ultimate purpose and impact the organization aims to achieve, while **goals** outline measurable objectives that guide progress toward that vision.

Key Components

- **Vision Statement:** A forward-thinking declaration of what the business strives to become.
- **Long-Term Impact**: The broader change or contribution the business hopes to make in its industry or community.
- **Strategic Goals**: Specific, actionable targets that drive business success.
- **Short-Term Milestones**: Immediate objectives that help measure progress.
- **Alignment & Adaptability**: Ensuring goals support the vision while allowing flexibility for evolving business needs.

Clarifying the Business Idea and Long-Term Vision

Clarifying a business idea and long-term vision involves defining the core purpose, value, and strategic direction of a business. It ensures entrepreneurs have a clear roadmap for growth, impact, and sustainability.

Key Components

- **Business Idea**: A well-defined concept that addresses a specific market need and offers a unique value proposition.
- **Target Audience**: Identifying the customers who benefit from the business.
- **Mission Statement**: A concise declaration of what the business aims to achieve.
- **Long-Term Vision**: A future-oriented goal that outlines where the business wants to be in 5, 10, or 20 years.
- **Strategic Goals**: Actionable steps for growth, innovation, and market positioning.
- **Adaptability**: Ensuring the business evolves with industry changes and customer demands.

To clarify your business idea and long-term vision, consider these key points:

- **A) Business Idea**

  - **What problems are you solving?** Clearly define the pain points your business addresses for new patrons.

Notes:_____

_____
_____
_____
_____
_____
_____
_____
_____
_____
_____
_____
_____
_____
_____
_____
_____
_____
_____
_____
_____
_____
_____
_____
_____
_____
_____
_____
_____
_____
_____

- **Target audience:** Who are the patrons that will benefit from your services or platform?

Notes:

- **Unique value proposition:** What makes your idea stand out, and why is it better than what's already out there?
It's all about explaining why your approach is special and why people should choose it over other options.

    Notes:_____

- **Key offerings:** What are you giving people—help, service, knowledge, money, or a supportive community?

  It's all about letting people know exactly what they can get from you.

Notes:

B) **Long-Term Vision**

- **Growth strategy:** Where do you see your business in the future, 5, 10 even 20 years—getting bigger, teaming up with others, or offering more services? It's all about describing your long-term plan and how you'll grow over time.

Notes:

- **Sustainability:** How will your business keep up with changes and stay strong, even when the market shifts?
  It's all about making sure you're flexible, ready to grow, and able to handle new challenges

Notes:_____

- **Legacy:** What mark do you want your business to leave behind—helping people, changing an industry, or making life better in some way?
  It's all about the big, lasting impact your business will have even after you're gone.

Notes:_____

Identifying Key Goals and Objectives for Success

Identifying key goals and objectives is the process of establishing clear, measurable targets that guide an organization toward achieving its mission. Goals define broad aspirations, while objectives outline specific actions to accomplish them.

Key Elements of Success Goals and Objectives

- **Clarity & Alignment:** Your business goals should match the big-picture mission and vision—everything should work together toward the same purpose. It's about making sure every decision helps move your business in the right direction.

    "How do my business goals support and reinforce the core mission and vision, and what adjustments are necessary to ensure long-term alignment?

Notes:_____
_____
_____
_____
_____
_____
_____
_____
_____
_____
_____
_____
_____
_____
_____
_____
_____
_____
_____
_____
_____
_____

- **Measurability:** Goals should have clear numbers so you can see if you're making progress. It's about setting specific targets—like growing by 20%, gaining 1,000 new customers, or hitting sales goals so you know if you're on track.

    "How can I define measurable objectives that allow me to track progress, make data-driven decisions, and ensure continuous improvement?"

Notes:

- **Time-Bound Targets:** Give your goals a deadline so you stay on track and are responsible for getting them done. It's all about setting clear time limits—like finishing a project in 3 months or reaching 1,000 sales in a year—so progress stays focused.

    "How can you establish realistic deadlines for your objectives to maintain accountability and drive consistent progress?"

Notes:

- **Actionable Steps:** Every goal should have a step-by-step plan to make it happen. It's all about breaking big ideas into smaller tasks so you know exactly what to do next.

    "What specific steps and resources are needed to successfully execute each objective, and how can I ensure progress stays on track?"

Notes;_____

- **Adaptability:** Your goals should be flexible so you can adjust when things change. It's all about making sure your plans can shift if needed—whether it's changing strategies, updating timelines, or trying new approaches to stay on track.

    "How can I structure my goals and objectives to remain adaptable to unexpected changes while staying aligned with my business vision?"

Notes:_____
_____
_____
_____
_____
_____
_____
_____
_____
_____
_____
_____
_____
_____
_____
_____
_____
_____
_____
_____
_____
_____
_____
_____
_____
_____
_____

Truism #1

"The journey ahead often requires revisiting the roots that first gave you the foundation."

"This is what the Lord says: 'Stand at the crossroads and look; ask for the ancient paths, ask where the good way is, and walk in it, and you will find rest for your souls" Jeremiah 6:16.

This verse highlights the importance of reflecting on foundational truths and past wisdom to move forward in the right direction. Sometimes, revisiting where we started helps us gain clarity for the future.

Reflection:

_____
_____
_____
_____
_____
_____
_____
_____
_____
_____
_____
_____
_____
_____
_____
_____
_____
_____

Chapter 2
Market Research & Competitive Analysis

Market Research and Competitive Analysis

Involve gathering data on industry trends, consumer behavior, and competitors to make informed business decisions. These processes help businesses identify opportunities, risks, and strategies for gaining a competitive advantage. By conducting thorough market research and competitive analysis, businesses can better understand their industry landscape and develop strategies for sustainable growth.

Key Components

- **Market Research**

    Identifies target customers, demographics, and buying habits. It's all about understanding the people who will buy from you, so you can meet their needs and make smart business decisions.

    Analyzes industry trends and market demand. Studying the market to see what's popular and what people want to buy. It's all about spotting trends and understanding demand so you can make smarter business decisions. Researching customer feedback and behaviors to see what competitors are doing well and where your business can improve. It's all about spotting trends, listening to customers, and making changes that keep them happy and coming back.

    Assesses customer needs and preferences. Figuring out what customers want, what they like, and what keeps them coming back. It's all about understanding their needs and preferences so you can offer products or services they'll love. Finding gaps in the market that your business can fill. Spotting what's missing in the market and offering something unique to stand out. It's all about finding opportunities where customers aren't fully satisfied and giving them something better or different.

- **Competitive Analysis**

    Evaluates direct and indirect competitors. Checking out both obvious and hidden competitors to see what they're doing. It's all about understanding who your competition is, how they operate, and how you can stand out from the crowd. Identifying direct and indirect competitors and assessing their business models, pricing, and strategies. Look at all types of competitors to see what they sell, how they price things, and how they attract customers. It's all about understanding who you're up against and learning from their successes and mistakes to make your business stronger.

    Identify strengths, weaknesses, and unique value propositions of competitors. Look at what your competitors do well, where they struggle, and what makes them different. It's all about learning from their strengths, spotting their weaknesses, and figuring out how you can stand out. Clearly defining what sets your business apart, such as innovation, affordability, customer service, or product quality. What makes your business special—whether it's better prices, amazing service, unique products, or fresh ideas? It's all about showing why customers should choose you instead of the competition.

- **Helps refine pricing, marketing, and product positioning strategies.** Studying your competitors helps you set the right prices, market effectively, and position your product in a way that stands out. It's all about learning from others so you can make smarter decisions and attract more customers. Understanding where competitors stand in the industry and how they attract their target audience. Figuring out where other businesses fit in the industry and how they win over customers. It's all about understanding their strengths, messaging, and strategies so you can position your business in the best possible way.

Notes:

Analyzing Industry Trends and Market Demand

Analyzing **industry trends** and **market demand** involves researching and interpreting patterns, consumer behavior, and competitive dynamics to make informed business decisions. This process helps businesses stay ahead of shifts in the market and identify opportunities for growth.

Key Components

- **Industry Trends:** Looking at new ideas, technologies, and what customers are starting to like. It's all about keeping up with changes so your business stays relevant and competitive.

  How does your business keep up with changes by spotting new ideas, using the latest technology, and understanding what customers want?

Notes:

- **Market Demand:** Assessing the need or desire for specific products or services. Figuring out what people want to buy and how much they need it. It's all about understanding demand so you can offer the right products or services at the right time.

  Have you effectively determined whether there is demand for your product or service before planning on launching it?

Notes:

- **Competitor Analysis:** Checking out other businesses to see what they do well, where they struggle, and what makes them different.
  It's all about learning from them so you can improve your own business and find ways to stand out.

  Have you taken a close look at any competitors to see what they do well, where they struggle, and what makes them different, so you can improve your own strategy?

Notes:_____
_____
_____
_____
_____
_____
_____
_____
_____
_____
_____
_____
_____
_____
_____
_____
_____
_____
_____
_____
_____
_____
_____
_____
_____
_____
_____
_____

- **Economic and Social Factors:** Looking at things like money, changing trends, and rules that affect businesses. It's all about understanding how the economy, culture, and laws shape industries and customer behavior.

    How can your business keep up with changes in the economy, shifts in culture, and new government rules to stay strong and successful?

Notes:_____

_____
_____
_____
_____
_____
_____
_____
_____
_____
_____
_____
_____
_____
_____
_____
_____
_____
_____
_____
_____
_____
_____
_____
_____
_____
_____

Data-Driven Insights: Using facts, numbers, and surveys to predict what customers will want in the future. It's all about studying data to make smarter decisions and stay ahead of trends.

How can your business use reports, customer surveys, and data to spot future trends and figure out what people want, so you can make better decisions?

Notes:_____

Truism #2

"Plans can change – don't rely on what hasn't happened yet."

"Do not boast about tomorrow, for you do not know what a day may bring." Proverbs 27:1

This verse reminds us to be cautious about assuming outcomes too soon. It encourages patience and wisdom, ensuring that we wait for things to fully unfold before celebrating or making decisions.

Reflection:

Chapter 3

Business Structure & Legal Setup

The business Structure and Legal Setup

Starting a business the right way means following certain legal steps. You need to pick a business type that suits your goals, register with the proper authorities, and meet all legal requirements. Some businesses go beyond just making money—they aim to improve a community, industry, or the environment. These types of businesses focus on making a positive impact while still following the necessary legal guidelines.

Key Components

- **Business Structure:**
  Sole Proprietorship – A business run by one person who makes all the decisions and takes full responsibility for everything, including debts. It's the simplest setup—easy to start, but it means you're personally responsible for any risks.

  Partnership – A business owned by two or more people who share responsibilities, profits, and risks. It's a team effort—partners work together and split the benefits, but they also share the challenges.

  Liability Company (LLC) – An LLC mixes features of corporations and partnerships, giving business owners legal protection from personal liability. It's a flexible structure—owners aren't personally responsible for business debts, but they still control how the company runs.

  Corporation – A corporation is its own separate entity, meaning the business—not the owners—is responsible for debts and legal issues. It's a structured setup that offers strong liability protection, so personal assets stay safe if the company runs into trouble.

- **Legal Setup**
  Business Registration – Making your business official by signing up with the government. It's all about registering your company with state and federal agencies so you can operate legally.

Licenses & Permits – Getting the right approvals to legally run your business. It's all about making sure you have the necessary licenses and permits to follow industry rules and avoid legal trouble.

Tax Identification Number (EIN) – An EIN is a special number businesses need for taxes and hiring workers. It's like a business's Social Security number—it helps the government track tax filings and lets companies legally hire employees.

Contracts & Agreements – Making official agreements so everything runs smoothly and legally. It's all about creating contracts for partnerships, business operations, and customer transactions to avoid misunderstandings and protect everyone involved.

Compliance & Liability Protection – Making sure your business follows all the rules to stay legal and avoid trouble. It's all about complying with state and federal laws so you don't face fines, lawsuits, or shutdowns.

Determining the Appropriate Business Entity

Starting a business means making key legal and financial decisions. You need to pick the right business type, register it properly, and follow the rules to stay compliant. The type of business you choose affects taxes, liability, ownership, and how much control you have over operations. Simply put, these steps help set up your business in the right way so it can run smoothly and legally.

Common Business Entities & Their Characteristics:

Sole Proprietorship

- Owned and operated by one person.
- Simple setup with minimal paperwork.
- Full personal liability for business debts and obligations.
- Taxed as personal income of the owner.

Partnership

- **General Partnership (GP)** – Shared liability and management among partners.
- **Limited Partnership (LP)** – One general partner with full control, others with limited liability.
- **Limited Liability Partnership (LLP)** – Protects all partners from personal liability.
- Profits and losses pass through to partners' personal tax returns.

Limited Liability Company (LLC)

- Combines aspects of corporations and sole proprietorships.
- Owners (members) have liability protection.
- Flexible taxation – can be taxed as a sole proprietorship, partnership, or corporation.
- Fewer formalities compared to corporations.

Corporation

- **C Corporation** – Separate legal entity, shareholders have limited liability.
- **S Corporation** – Similar to C Corp but allows pass-through taxation.
- **Benefit Corporation (B Corp)** – Focuses on social and environmental impact alongside profit.
- Requires more regulations and paperwork.

Factors to Consider When Choosing a Business Entity

- **Liability Protection** – Deciding how much personal responsibility you want if your business runs into legal or financial trouble. It's all about choosing the right setup to protect your personal assets in case something goes wrong.

Notes:

- **Taxation** – Decide whether your business income is taxed as part of your personal earnings or separately. It's all about choosing the right tax setup—some businesses pay taxes through their owners, while others are taxed separately as their own entity.

Notes:

- **Ownership Structure** – Decide if you want to run the business by yourself or share ownership with others. It's all about choosing between full control or working with partners or investors who have a stake in the business.

Notes:_____

- **Management Overhead** – Think about how much paperwork, rules, and government requirements you can handle. It's all about choosing a business setup that matches your ability to manage legal and administrative tasks without feeling overwhelmed.

Notes:

- **Growth Plans** – Do you want to bring in investors or grow your business in a big way? It's all about deciding whether you need outside funding or if you'll expand using your own resources.

Notes:_____

Necessary Permits, Licenses, and Compliance Requirements

To keep a business legal and avoid trouble, you need to get the right permits and licenses and follow the rules. These steps help protect the business, prevent fines, and make customers and partners trust you. It's all about staying on the right side of the law while building a solid reputation.

Key Components

Business Licenses & Permits

- **General Business License** – Required for most businesses to operate legally within a city or county.

- **Industry-Specific Permits** – Depending on the type of business (e.g., food service, construction, healthcare), additional permits may be required.

- **Zoning & Land Use Permits** – Necessary if running a business from a physical location.

- **Sales Tax Permit** – Required for businesses selling taxable goods or services.

- **Tax Identification Number (EIN)** - Required for tax filling and hiring employees.

Compliance Requirements

- **Federal & State Regulations** – Businesses must adhere to industry laws, such as safety regulations (OSHA), environmental guidelines (EPA), or financial compliance standards.

- **Employment Laws** – If hiring employees, compliance with labor laws, wage requirements, and workplace safety is necessary.

- **Data Protection & Privacy Laws** – If handling customer information, businesses must follow cybersecurity and privacy regulations.

- **Contracts & Liability Protection** – Legal agreements, insurance policies, and intellectual property protection to mitigate risks.

Notes:

Truism #3

"Every moment serves a purpose-trust the timing"

"To everything there is a season, and a time to every purpose under the heaven"
Ecclesiastes 3:1

This verse beautifully expresses the idea that life unfolds in seasons, each with its own purpose and timing. It reminds us to trust the process and embraces the changes that come our way.

Reflection:

___

Chapter 4

Financial Planning & Budgeting

Financial Planning and Budgeting

Keeping a business financially strong means handling money wisely. That includes predicting income, keeping expenses in check, and setting clear financial goals. Good budgeting and planning help a business stay stable, grow, and prepare for the future. In short, smart money management keeps a business running smoothly and ready for success.

Key Components

- **Financial Planning**

    Short-Term and long-term financial goals. It's all about figuring out how much you need to spend, save, and invest so your business stays strong today and keeps growing over time.

    Forecasting income, expenses, and profitability. It's all about estimating future income, planning expenses, and figuring out whether your business will be profitable over time.

    Creating a strategy for funding, Investments, and business expansion. It's all about figuring out where funding will come from, how to use investments effectively, and making smart choices to expand successfully.

- **Budgeting**

    Allocating resources efficiently based on business priorities. It's all about deciding where to put funds so every dollar helps the business grow and succeed.

    Monitoring cash flow to avoid overspending or financial risk. It's all about making sure there's enough cash to cover expenses while avoiding financial trouble.

    Establishing contingency plans for unexpected financial challenges. It's all about preparing for financial surprises, like sudden expenses or a drop in income, so your business can stay afloat even in tough times.

Creating a Startup Budget and Financial Projections

A startup budget is basically a money plan for a new business. It lists the costs of getting started and keeping things running. Financial projections help predict how much money the business will make, spend, and keep as profit. This planning helps entrepreneurs stay on track, grow, and make sure their business survives long term.

Key Components of a Startup Budget

- **Initial Costs** – Expenses for registration, equipment, inventory, branding, and legal fees.

    What are the required registration fees for establishing your business?

Notes:_____

What equipment will you need to start, and how much will it cost?

Notes:

How much inventory do you need upfront, and what are the sourcing costs?

Notes:

What expenses are involved in developing your brand (logo, website, marketing materials)?

Notes:

Are there any legal fees, including business licensing, contracts, or professional consultations?

Notes:

Will you need office space or a storefront, and what are the rental or purchase costs?

Notes:

Are there any hidden startup costs you should prepare for (insurance, permits, software)?

Notes:

What is your total estimated budget for initial costs, and how will you finance them?

Notes:

- **Operating Expenses** – Recurring costs like rent, utilities, salaries, marketing, and software subscriptions.

    What are the monthly rent costs for your office, storefront, or workspace?

Notes:

What utilities (electricity, water, internet, etc.) do you need, and what are their estimated costs?

Notes:

How much will you allocate for employee salaries and benefits?

Notes:

What recurring marketing expenses (advertising, promotions, social media management) will be required?

Notes:

What software or technology tools do you need, and what are the subscription costs?

Notes:

Do you have insurance, licensing renewals, or other regulatory expenses to account for?

Notes:

What costs will be associated with maintaining inventory, supplies, and equipment?

Notes:

How will operating expenses fluctuate seasonally or as your business grows?

Notes:

- **Emergency Fund** – A reserve for unexpected expenses or financial downturns.

    How much should you set aside to cover unexpected expenses?

Notes:

What types of emergencies might arise (equipment failure, unexpected repairs, revenue loss)?

Notes:

How many months of operating expenses do you want your emergency fund to cover?

Notes:

Do you have a plan for replenishing the fund if it gets used?

Notes:

Where will you store the emergency fund (separate account, investment fund)?

Notes:

How will you determine when it's necessary to use emergency savings versus other financial resources?

Notes:

What strategies can you implement to minimize financial risks and avoid relying heavily on emergency savings?

Notes:

- **Break-Even Analysis** – The moment when your business makes enough money to cover all its costs—without profit or loss. It's all about figuring out when your income matches expenses, so you know the minimum sales needed to stay afloat

    What are your total fixed costs (rent, salaries, insurance, etc.)?

Notes:

What are your variable costs per unit (materials, production, shipping)?

Notes:

What is your product or service's selling price per unit?

Notes:

How many units or services do you need to sell to cover all costs?

Notes:

What is your break-even point in terms of revenue?

Notes:

How long will it take to reach this break-even point based on projected sales?

Notes:

What are some simple ways to spend less money and make more profit in your business?

Notes:

How will market fluctuations or unexpected expenses affect your break-even timeline?

Notes:

Financial Projections

- **Revenue Forecast** – Estimating sales based on market research and pricing strategy. It's all about using research to estimate future sales and adjusting prices to maximize profits.

How much money do you think your business will make each month and year, based on how many people want your product or service?

Notes:

How does the way you set prices change how much money your business makes?

Notes:

How much do you want to sell in your first year, and how does that compare to what similar businesses usually achieve?

Notes:

- **Expense Estimates** – Predicting monthly and annual costs.

    What are your projected monthly operating expenses (rent, utilities, salaries, marketing, etc.)?

Notes:

How will your annual costs compare to monthly expenses (seasonal variations, tax obligations, insurance renewals)?

Notes:

How much of your business income will be spent on regular expenses versus costs that change based on sales?

Notes:

- **Cash Flow Projection** – Tracking expected inflows and outflows to maintain financial stability.

    What are your estimated monthly inflows (sales, investments, loans, grants)?

Notes:

What are your projected monthly outflows (rent, salaries, inventory, marketing, utilities)?

Notes:

How will seasonal trends affect your cash flow stability?

Notes:

- **Profitability Analysis** – Assessing when the business will become profitable.

    At what point will revenue exceed total costs, making the business profitable?

Notes:

What is your projected timeline for reaching profitability?

Notes:_____

How does the way you set prices and spend money change how much profit your business makes?

Notes:

Exploring Funding Options (Loans, Investors, Grants)

Starting a business takes money, and there are different ways to get it. Entrepreneurs can look at options like loans, investors, crowdfunding, or personal savings to help fund their startup. The right choice depends on how much money you will need, your financial situation, and your plans for the future. It's all about finding the best way to support the business and keep it growing

Key Funding Sources

Loans

- **Bank Loans** – Traditional loans from banks requiring credit approval and repayment terms.

- **Small Business Administration (SBA) Loans** – Government-backed loans with favorable rates.

- **Microloans** – Small-scale loans ideal for startups with limited capital needs.

- **Lines of Credit** – Flexible borrowing options where businesses can withdraw funds as needed.

Investors

- **Angel Investors** – are people who give money to startups in return for a share of the business or a future option to convert their investment into ownership. They help new businesses get off the ground and grow while hoping to make a profit when the company succeeds.

- **Venture Capital (VC) Firms** – give money to startups that have big growth potential. They invest in businesses that can expand quickly and become highly profitable. In return, they usually get ownership in the company and hope to make a large profit as the business succeeds.

- **Crowdfunding** – when a lot of people each chip in small amounts of money to support a startup or project. Entrepreneurs use platforms like Kickstarter or Indiegogo to get funding from backers who believe in their idea. It's a way to raise money without relying on big investors or banks.

- **Private Equity** – big investment firms put money into established businesses that want to grow. These firms help companies expand in exchange for ownership or profits down the line. It's a way for businesses to get funding without going public or taking on traditional loans.

Grants & Alternative Funding

- **Government Grants** – Non-repayable funds from agencies supporting small businesses and innovation. (**Small Business Innovation Research (SBIR) program or State Trade Expansion Program (STEP).**

- **Startup Competitions & Incubators** – Programs offering funding, mentorship, and networking opportunities. (**Startup World Cup or Y Combinator**).

- **Nonprofit & Industry-Specific Grants** – Targeted funding for businesses in healthcare, education, sustainability, and more. (**Ford Foundation Grants or National Endowment for the Arts (NEA) Grants**).

- **Revenue-Based Financing** – Investors fund a business in exchange for a percentage of future revenue instead of equity. **(Lighter Capital)**

Notes:

Truism #4

"You've already been equipped, trust in what He's placed within you."

"His divine power has given us everything we need for a godly life through our knowledge of him who called us by his own glory and goodness." 2 Peter 1:3

This verse reminds us that God has already equipped us with the tools, wisdom, and strength necessary to fulfill our purpose- we just need to trust and act on it.

Reflection:

_____
_____
_____
_____
_____
_____
_____
_____
_____
_____
_____
_____
_____
_____
_____
_____
_____
_____
_____

Chapter 5

Branding & Marketing Strategy

Branding and Marketing Strategy refers to the process of establishing a strong identity for a business and effectively promoting it to the target audience. A well-crafted strategy helps businesses build recognition, trust, and customer engagement.

Key Components

Branding:

- **Branding Identity -** Defines the logo, colors, typography, and overall visual style.

- **Brand Voice & Messaging –** Creates a consistent tone and communication style.

- **Unique Value Proposition (UVP) –** Clarifies what sets the brand apart from competitors.

- **Brand Story –** Establishes an emotional connection with the audience.

Marketing Strategy:

- **Target Audience Analysis –** Identifies customer demographics, needs, and preferences.

- **Marketing Channels –** Utilizes social media. Email campaigns, SEO, and advertising.

- **Content Strategy –** Develops engaging materials like blogs, videos, and promotional graphics.

- **Customer Engagement & Retention –** Builds loyalty through personalized outreach, offers, and community interactions.

- **Performance Measurement –** Tracks metrics such as conversion rates, engagement, and return on investment (ROI).

Developing Brand Identity (Name, Logo, Messaging)

Brand identity is the visual, verbal, and emotional representation of a business. It defines how a company presents itself and how it resonates with its audience.

Key Components

Name

- It should be memorable, unique, and relevant to your industry.
- It must be easy to pronounce and spell for brand recognition.
- Can reflect your business values, mission, or personality.
- Check for domain availability if you plan to establish an online presence.

Logo & Visual Elements

- A strong logo should be **simple, adaptable, and visually appealing**.
- Consider **color psychology**—colors influence emotions and perceptions.
- Typography and design choices should reflect **your brand's personality** (e.g., modern, playful, professional).
- Ensure it looks great across various platforms, from websites to social media and packaging.

Messaging & Voice

- Develop a **brand story** that connects emotionally with your audience.
- Define your **tone of voice**—whether formal, friendly, inspirational, or authoritative.
- Create a compelling **tagline or slogan** that captures your brand's essence.
- Consistency in messaging builds **trust and recognition** over time.

Notes:

Outlining Marketing Channels (Social Media, Website, Advertising)

Marketing channels are the **platforms and methods** businesses use to promote their brand, reach their target audience, and drive customer engagement. Selecting the right mix of marketing channels ensures **effective outreach and visibility**.

Key Marketing Channels

Social Media Marketing

- Platforms like **Facebook, Instagram, LinkedIn, Twitter, TikTok** for brand awareness.
- **Content strategies** include organic posts, paid promotions, influencer partnerships, and community engagement.
- Ideal for building relationships, engaging directly with customers, and storytelling.

Website & SEO

- A professional website serves as a **central hub** for brand identity, information, and transactions.
- **Search Engine Optimization (SEO)** helps improve visibility on Google and other search engines.
- Blogs, landing pages, and multimedia content enhance customer experience and lead generation.

Paid Advertising

- **Google Ads, Facebook Ads, LinkedIn Ads** help businesses reach target audiences.
- **Pay-Per-Click (PPC)** campaigns ensure businesses pay only for user engagement.
- **Display ads, retargeting, and sponsored content** enhance brand recognition.

Email Marketing & Outreach

- **Newsletters and automated email sequences** help retain customers and nurture leads.
- Personalized emails with **discounts, updates, and promotions** boost engagement.
- **Cold outreach & partnerships** expand networking opportunities.

Offline Marketing Channels

- Events, trade shows, printed materials, and direct mail campaigns help **reach local audiences**.
- Public relations strategies, press releases, and media partnerships establish credibility.
- Networking and word-of-mouth recommendations remain powerful tools.

Notes:

Truism #5

"Success requires effort – nothing comes without work"

For even when we were with you, we gave you this rule: "The one who is unwilling to work shall not eat" 2 Thessalonians 3:10.

This verse emphasizes the importance of effort and responsibility – if we want to receive something, we must be willing to put in the work. It reinforces the idea that rewards come through diligence and commitment.

Reflection:

Chapter 6

Operational Planning & Logistics

Operational Planning and Logistics Involve designing and managing the processes required to efficiently run a business. This ensures smooth daily operations, optimized resources allocation, and effective supply chain management.

Key Components

Operational Planning:

- **Strategic Objectives –** Defining key business goal and aligning operations to meet them.

    What are the top three long-term goals for your business?

Notes:

How do your strategic objectives help turn your mission into action and bring your vision to life?

Notes:

What specific actions need to be taken to achieve each objective?

Notes:

- **Process Optimization –** Making work smoother and cheaper by organizing tasks better. It's all about finding ways to speed up processes, reduce wasted time, and cut costs while keeping everything running efficiently.

    Which workflows or processes are causing delays or inefficiencies?

Notes:_____

How can using technology or automated tools help make work faster and easier while saving money?

Notes:

What tasks can be eliminated, outsourced, or consolidated to reduce costs?

Notes:

Are your work processes set up in the smartest way, like top businesses in your industry, do it?

Notes:

Are employees equipped with the right tools and training to maximize efficiency?

Notes:

What feedback from customers or team members could help refine processes?

Notes:

How often should you check and improve your work processes to keep things running smoothly?

Notes:

- **Resource Management** – Making sure people, money, and equipment are used in the best way to keep things running smoothly. It's all about organizing resources wisely so everything is efficient, cost-effective, and supports business goals.

Where is the business spending its money, and how is it divided between different areas?

Notes:

Is your team being used in the best way, or do you need more people in certain areas?

Notes:

What are some simple ways to help your team work efficiently and get more done?

Notes:

How can using technology and automated tools help make the best use of people, money, and equipment in a business?

Notes:

Are physical resources (equipment, office space, inventory) being used efficiently?

Notes:

How can your business spend less money while still running smoothly and staying successful?

Notes:

How does the way you work with suppliers and vendors affect how well you utilize your people, money, and equipment?

Notes:

- **Risk Management –** Spotting possible problems early and making backup plans to handle them. It's all about preparing for risks before they happen so your business stays strong and avoids major setbacks

    What potential challenges or risks could affect your business operations?

Notes:_____

_____
_____
_____
_____
_____
_____
_____
_____
_____
_____
_____
_____
_____
_____
_____
_____
_____
_____
_____
_____
_____
_____
_____
_____
_____
_____
_____
_____

How will shifts in the economy, changing prices, or moves by your competitors affect how well your business does?

Notes:

How do you keep your business information safe from hackers and other online threats?

Notes:

Are there any legal or compliance rules you need to follow to keep your business safe?

Notes:

What money problems might come up, and how will you prevent them from hurting your business?

Notes:

How will unexpected disruptions (supply chain delays, natural disasters, staff shortages) be handled?

Notes:

Do you have contingency plans in place for worst-case scenarios?

Notes:

How frequently will you review and update your risk management strategies?

Notes:

Logistics:

- **Supply Chain Coordination –** Keeping track of products, buying supplies, and making sure items get where they need to go efficiently. It's all about making sure the right stuff is available at the right time while keeping costs down and deliveries smooth.

    How will you manage inventory to avoid shortages or overstocking?

Notes:_____

What are the best ways to buy supplies quickly and affordably without wasting money or causing delays?

Notes:

How will you establish relationships with reliable suppliers and vendors?

Notes:

What's the best way to move products quickly and smoothly from suppliers to customers without delays or extra costs?

Notes:

How will you track and monitor supply chain performance?

Notes:

What technology or software can help streamline inventory and procurement processes?

Notes:

What contingency plans do you have in place for supply chain disruptions?

Notes:

How will you ensure quality control throughout the supply chain?

Notes:

- **Transportation & Delivery** – Ensuring timely and cost-effective movement of goods and services.

    What is the most cost-effective and reliable method for transporting your goods or services?

Notes:_____

How will you ensure timely deliveries to customers or distribution centers?

Notes:

What things make shipping more expensive, like gas prices, travel distance, and deals with delivery companies?

Notes:

Do you need to work with third-party delivery services, or will you manage transportation in-house?

Notes:

How will you keep track of deliveries to make sure they arrive on time and keep customers happy?

Notes:

What contingency plans do you have for delays, lost shipments, or unexpected disruptions?

Notes:

What's the best way to plan routes and schedules so deliveries are fast but don't cost too much?

Notes:

What tools or software can make shipping easier and help ensure packages arrive on time?

Notes:

- **Technology Integration –** Using smart tools and software to make work easier, faster, and more efficient. It's all about letting technology handle repetitive tasks so businesses can focus on bigger goals.

  What tasks can be automated to improve efficiency and reduce manual workload?

Notes:_____

_____
_____
_____
_____
_____
_____
_____
_____
_____
_____
_____
_____
_____
_____
_____
_____
_____
_____
_____
_____
_____
_____
_____
_____

What software solutions can help businesses keep track of money, stock, and customers more easily and efficiently?

Notes:

How can technology enhance customer experience and engagement?

Notes:

What cybersecurity measures need to be implemented to protect business data?

Notes:

What special tools or software are made for your industry that can help work get done faster and more smoothly?

Notes:

Will adding new technology make things more expensive, or will it help save money in the long run?

Notes:

What training or support is needed for employees to effectively use new software?

Notes:

Will new technology keep up as your business grows and changes, or will you need to upgrade later?

Notes:

- **Customer Fulfillment** – Setting up processes to make sure customers get what they need easily and without hassle. It's all about making service smooth, reliable, and keeping customers happy.

    What systems or processes ensure timely and accurate order fulfillment?

Notes:

How can technology be used to improve service delivery and customer experience?

Notes:

What strategies will you implement to handle customer inquiries and complaints efficiently?

Notes:

How will you maintain quality control and consistency in your products or services?

Notes:

What metrics will you use to measure customer satisfaction and fulfillment success?

Notes:

How can you streamline shipping, packaging, and delivery to enhance efficiency?

Notes:

What contingency plans do you have for delays, damaged goods, or service disruptions?

Notes:

How will you personalize and optimize customer interactions to build loyalty and trust?

Notes:

Establishing Workflows, Suppliers, and Technological Needs

Setting up efficient workflows, selecting reliable suppliers, and integrating the right technology ensures seamless business operations and long-term success.

Key Components

Workflows 🛠

- **Process Mapping:** Figuring out what needs to be done and setting up clear steps to get it done smoothly. It's all about breaking work into manageable parts so tasks flow easily from start to finish.

- **Automation & Efficiency:** Use smart tools to handle repetitive work automatically so everything gets done faster and more smoothly. It's all about making work easier and boosting productivity by letting technology do the boring stuff.

- **Role Assignments:** Give different tasks to the right people so everything runs smoothly and gets done efficiently. It's all about making sure everyone knows their role and workflows without hiccups.

- **Quality Control:** Set clear standards to measure how well things are running and keep everything consistent. It's all about checking the quality of work regularly so it stays reliable and meets expectations.

Suppliers & Vendors 🚚

- **Supplier Research:** Check prices, quality, and trustworthiness before picking a supplier. It's all about finding the right balance between affordability, good products, and reliable service.

- **Contracts & Agreements:** Clearly set rules for costs, delivery schedules, and what's expected in a deal. It's all about making sure both sides agree on fair terms, so everything runs smoothly without confusion.

- **Inventory Management:** Figure out how much stock you need based on future demand, so you don't run out or have too much. It's all about balancing supply and demand to keep things running smoothly without wasting money or missing sales.

- **Backup Suppliers:** Find extra suppliers so you're covered if something goes wrong with your main one. It's all about having backup options to keep things running smoothly without delays or shortages

Technological Needs

- **Software & Tools:** Pick the right apps to help manage money, organize projects, connect with customers, and promote your business.

- **Cybersecurity Measures**: Keep data safe and follow privacy rules to protect important information. It's all about using security tools and good practices to prevent hacks and make sure personal and business data stays secure.

- **Cloud Solutions:** Use online storage and software to grow your business and work from anywhere. It's all about keeping data safe, expanding easily, and staying connected no matter where you are.

- **Infrastructure & Hardware:** Figure out what basic equipment you need, like computers, payment systems, and storage, to keep everything running smoothly. It's all about making sure your business has the right tools to operate efficiently and grow.

Notes:

Hiring Needs and Employee Management Strategies

Hiring needs and employee management strategies involve identifying workforce requirements, recruiting the right talent, and implementing systems to foster productivity, engagement, and retention. This ensures a business operates efficiently while maintaining a positive work culture.

Key Components

Hiring Needs

- **Job Roles & Responsibilities** – Define essential positions based on business functions.

- **Skills & Qualifications** – Identify expertise needed for long-term success.

- **Workforce Planning** – Forecast hiring needs as the business scales.

- **Recruitment Methods** – Utilize job postings, networking, referrals, and hiring platforms.

- **Budget Considerations** – Plan salaries, benefits, and training costs.

Management Strategies

- **Onboarding & Training** – Establish structured orientation programs for new hires.

- **Performance Evaluation** – Implement systems to track employee growth and productivity.

- **Workplace Culture & Engagement** – Foster a supportive environment with recognition programs and incentives.

- **Conflict Resolution & Communication** – Ensure clear policies for addressing workplace issues.

- **Retention Strategies** – Promote career development opportunities and benefits that enhance job satisfaction.

Notes:

Truism #6

"No one else holds the key to your success – you do."

"Commit to the Lord whatever you do, and he will establish your plans." Proverbs 16:3.

This verse emphasizes personal responsibility and faith – success comes when we take initiative, trust in God, and actively pursue our goals rather than waiting for others to guide us.

Reflection:

Chapter 7

Launch Plans & Next Steps

Launch Plans and Next Steps is a structured roadmap for introducing a new business, product, or service to the market. It outlines key actions, timelines, and resources required for a successful launch. Next steps refer to follow-up actions necessary for growth and sustainability after the initial launch.

Key Components of a Launch Plan

- **Pre-Launch Preparation:** Finalizing branding, Marketing, and operational details.
- **Target Audience Engagement:** Building anticipation through promotions, social media, and outreach.
- **Go-to-Market Strategy:** Selecting the right distribution channels and launch tactics.
- **Execution & Timing:** Coordinating launch events, content, and advertisements.
- **Feedback Collection:** Monitoring customer responses and adjusting strategies as needed.

Next Steps for Growth & Sustainability

- **Performance Review:** review looks at how well a business is doing. It checks sales figures, how customers interact with the brand, and what people think about it. This helps businesses understand what's working, what's not, and how to improve.
- **Business Scaling:** growing a company by adding more products or services, teaming up with new partners, and reaching more customers. It's all about making the business bigger and more successful without losing quality or efficiency.
- **Customer Retention:** keeping customers coming back. Businesses use different strategies like great customer service, special deals, and regular communication to keep people engaged and loyal. The goal is to make sure customers stay happy and continue choosing the business instead of going elsewhere.
- **Operational Refinements:** making business processes better based on early feedback and what's been learned. It's about fixing what doesn't work, improving efficiency, and adjusting strategies to keep things running smoothly and successfully.
- **Long-Term Vision Alignment:** making sure a business's growth plans stay on track with its overall goals. It's about keeping expansion, investments, and strategies focused on what the company wants to achieve in the future, so everything moves in the right direction.

Setting Realistic Timelines for Launching

Establishing realistic timelines for a business launch involves **carefully planning tasks, allocating resources, and ensuring readiness** before officially entering the market. A well-structured timeline helps businesses stay organized, avoid delays, and manage expectations effectively.

Key Components

Pre-Launch Preparation (3-6 Months Before Launch)

- Finalize branding, business entity, and legal requirements.
- Develop a minimum viable product (MVP) or service prototype.
- Research competitors and refine marketing strategies.
- Build social media presence and generate early brand awareness.

Execution Phase (1-2 Months Before Launch)

- Begin promotional campaigns (email marketing, paid ads, influencer outreach).
- Conduct final testing of products, services, and customer workflows.
- Train staff and prepare for customer engagement.
- Secure necessary funding and finalize partnerships.

Official Launch (Launch Week & Month)

- Announce launch through events, PR campaigns, and online promotions.
- Actively engage with customers and collect feedback.
- Monitor sales, website traffic, and marketing performance.
- Address unexpected challenges and refine strategies accordingly.

Post-Launch Optimization (1-6 Months After Launch)

- Adjust operations based on feedback and customer trends.
- Expand marketing efforts and explore additional growth opportunities.
- Strengthening customer retention strategies and community engagement
- Evaluate financial performance and scale business accordingly.

Notes:

Creating Action Steps for the First Few Months of Business Operation

Establishing clear **action steps** in the initial months of business operation ensures stability, efficiency, and growth. A structured plan helps businesses refine workflows, build brand awareness, and generate early revenue.

Key Action Steps (First 3-6 Months)

Operational Setup & Refinement

- Finalize business registration, legal compliance, and permits.
- Set up accounting systems for tracking expenses and revenue.
- Establish reliable workflows and operational procedures.
- Organize inventory, suppliers, and technology integration.

Branding & Marketing Execution

- Launch website and optimize search engines (SEO).
- Build brand presence on social media and create engaging content.
- Run targeted advertising campaigns to attract first customers.
- Implement email marketing and customer outreach strategies.

Sales & Customer Engagement

- Develop introductory pricing, promotions, or early discounts.
- Build relationships with initial customers and gather feedback.
- Set up referral or loyalty programs to encourage repeat business.
- Track customer satisfaction and adjust business strategies accordingly.

Financial & Performance Analysis

- Monitor expenses, revenue, and cash flow.
- Evaluate marketing and sales performance metrics.
- Identify areas for cost savings and operational improvements.
- Prepare for scaling and potential funding opportunities.

Growth & Expansion Planning

- Refine business strategies based on real-world data and market response.
- Expand product or service offerings if demand supports growth.
- Strengthening partnerships and networking within the industry.
- Set long-term goals and adjust business objectives for sustainability.

Notes:

Truism #7

"Hard doesn't mean impossible – keep pushing forward."

"I have told you these things, so that in me you may have peace. In this world you will have trouble. But take care! I have overcome the world." John 16:33.

This verse acknowledges that life will be difficult, but it also offers encouragement – challenges are expected, yet with faith and perseverance, we can overcome them.

Reflection:

Chapter 8
Example
Business Idea

Business Name: ABC Meal Prep

Concept: A subscription-based meal prep service specializing in **healthy, organic, and customizable meal plans** for busy professionals and health-conscious individuals.

Market Need:

- Many individuals struggle with **meal planning, nutrition, and time constraints**.
- Demand for **affordable and convenient healthy eating solutions** continues to rise.
- Consumers seek **customized dietary options** such as keto, vegan, or high-protein meals.

Unique Value Proposition (UVP):

- **Fully customizable meal options** based on dietary preferences and health goals.
- **Locally sourced organic ingredients** to promote sustainability and freshness.
- **Convenient delivery model**—weekly meal kits sent directly to customers' doors.
- **AI-driven meal recommendations** that adjust plans based on customer feedback and nutritional needs.

This business idea solves a growing consumer challenge while standing out in the competitive meal prep industry through personalization, freshness, and tech-driven solutions.

Example
Market Research and Competitive Analysis

Let's say you're launching a new organic skincare brand. Before entering the market, you'd want to conduct market research and competitive analysis to understand industry trends, customer preferences, and existing competitors.

Example of Market Research:

- **Target Audience:** Research reveals that consumers aged 25-45, particularly those interested in sustainability, are most likely to buy organic skincare.

- **Consumer Preferences:** Surveys indicate that buyers prioritize ingredient transparency, eco-friendly packaging, and cruelty-free products.

- **Industry Trends:** Reports show a rising demand for clean beauty and an increasing interest in plant-based ingredients.

Example of Competitive Analysis:

- **Competitor Identification:** You identify top organic skincare brands such as ABC Harper and ABC Elephant.

- **Competitive Landscape:** Analyzing their strengths, weaknesses, pricing strategies, and customer reviews helps you understand market gaps.

- **Unique Selling Proposition (USP):** You discover that while competitors focus on luxury pricing, there's an opportunity to offer affordable yet high-quality organic skincare.

By leveraging both market research and competitive analysis, you'd be equipped to make informed decisions about pricing, branding, and product development, ensuring a strong entry into the market.

Example
Business Structure & Legal Setup

Business Name: ABC Consulting Group

Industry: Professional Services

Chosen Business Structure:

Limited Liability Company (LLC)

- ✅ Provides **liability protection**, separating personal assets from business debts.
- ✅ Allows **flexible taxation**—can be taxed as a sole proprietorship or corporation.
- ✅ Requires **less administrative paperwork** than a corporation.
- ✅ Offers **credibility and trust** to clients.

Legal Setup Steps Taken:

Business Registration: Filed LLC formation documents with the state.

Employer Identification Number (EIN): Applied for an EIN from the IRS for tax and payroll purposes.

Operating Agreement: Established internal rules for ownership structure and management.

Licenses & Permits: Secured industry-specific business licenses and professional certifications.

Tax Compliance: Registered with state and federal tax agencies for proper tax filings.

Contracts & Legal Agreements: Created client contracts, non-disclosure agreements (NDAs), and service agreements to protect business interests.

This structure provides **legal security, tax flexibility, and operational efficiency**, ensuring long-term success and protection for ABC Consulting Group.

Example
Financial Planning & Budgeting

Business Name: ABC Solutions

Industry: Technology & Software Development

Financial Plan Overview:

ABC Solutions aims to maintain financial stability while strategically investing in innovation and growth. The financial plan includes budgeting for operational expenses, revenue forecasting, and long-term investment strategies.

Startup Budget Breakdown:

Initial Costs:
- Business registration & legal setup – $2,500
- Office space & equipment – $10,000
- Website development – $3,500
- Marketing & advertising – $5,000
- Software development & testing – $15,000

Operating Expenses (Monthly):
- Employee salaries – $12,000
- Utilities & office maintenance – $2,000
- Subscription-based tools & software – $1,500
- Marketing campaigns – $3,000
- Miscellaneous expenses – $2,000

Financial Projections for First Year:

Revenue Forecast:
- Expected sales growth of **15% per quarter**.
- Monthly revenue target: **$25,000 in the first six months**, scaling up to **$50,000** by year-end.

Expense Management:
- Keeping operational costs below **60% of revenue** for profitability.
- Expanding through reinvestment in technology improvements.

Long-Term Financial Goals:
- ✅ Achieve profitability within 18 months.
- ✅ Secure additional funding for product expansion.
- ✅ Diversify revenue streams through subscription services and partnerships.

Example
Branding & Marketing Strategy

Business Name: ABC Skincare

Industry: Beauty & Wellness

Branding Strategy

- ✅ **Brand Identity:** Elegant, modern, and centered on luxury skincare solutions.
- ✅ **Brand Voice & Messaging:** Empowering, informative, and customer-focused.
- ✅ **Unique Value Proposition (UVP):** Clean, science-backed skincare tailored for glowing, healthy skin.
- ✅ **Logo & Design:** Soft pastel tones, sleek typography, and minimalist packaging to evoke sophistication.

Marketing Strategy

1. Digital Presence & Social Media

- Engage customers through **Instagram, TikTok, and Pinterest** with skincare tips & tutorials.
- Partner with **influencers & beauty experts** to build trust and credibility.
- Run **targeted ad campaigns** to reach skincare-conscious consumers.

2. Content Marketing & SEO

- Launch a **blog featuring skincare guides, ingredient education, and beauty trends.**
- Optimize website and product pages for **SEO to rank on Google searches.**
- Publish **video content** showcasing real results and testimonials.

3. Community Engagement & Customer Loyalty

- Introduce a **VIP rewards program** offering discounts & exclusive skincare consultations.
- Host **live Q&A sessions** and skincare challenges to increase engagement.
- Encourage user-generated content with **customer reviews and before-and-after photos.**

4. Strategic Partnerships & Retail Expansion

- Collaborate with **spas, dermatologists, and wellness brands** for product placement.
- Offer **subscription-based skincare boxes** for convenience.
- Expand to **high-end department stores and online marketplaces** for broader reach.

ABC Skincare's branding and marketing strategy ensures a strong presence in the beauty industry, fostering trust, engagement, and customer loyalty.

Example
Operational Planning & Logistics

Business Name: ABC Organic Market

Industry: Grocery & Food Retail

Operational Planning Strategy 📈

✅ **Inventory Management:** Implement a real-time tracking system to monitor stock levels and prevent shortages.

✅ **Supplier Relations:** Establish contracts with local farms and organic suppliers for consistent product availability.

✅ **Workflow Optimization:** Streamline processes for product receiving, stocking, and checkout efficiency.

✅ **Employee Roles & Training:** Define clear job descriptions and train staff in food handling, customer service, and order fulfillment.

✅ **Quality Control Measures:** Develop a system for inspecting perishable goods to ensure freshness and compliance with health regulations.

Logistics Management 🚚

✅ **Supply Chain Coordination:** Secure reliable distribution partners to transport organic products from suppliers to store locations.

✅ **Delivery & Fulfillment:** Introduce online ordering with eco-friendly home delivery services.

✅ **Technology Integration:** Use automated inventory systems and AI-driven demand forecasting for optimized stock management.

✅ **Customer Experience:** Ensure smooth checkout, convenient payment options, and excellent service for shoppers.

✅ **Sustainability Initiatives:** Implement waste reduction strategies, reusable packaging solutions, and energy-efficient operations.

This operational and logistics framework ensures ABC Organic Market runs smoothly while delivering high-quality organic products to customers efficiently.

Example
Launch Plan & Next Steps

Business Name: ABC Candles
Industry: Sustainable Home Goods

Launch Plan Strategy 🚀

☑ **Pre-Launch (3 Months Before Launch)**

- Finalize branding, packaging, and website setup.
- Conduct market research to refine product positioning.
- Build anticipation through social media teasers and influencer collaborations.
- Secure partnerships with local eco-friendly vendors and distributors.

☑ **Launch Week Execution** 🎉

- Host a virtual or in-person launch event showcasing the product.
- Roll out limited time offers to attract early customers.
- Implement PR and media outreach to generate buzz.
- Track sales and customer engagement to optimize launch strategies.

Next Steps for Growth & Expansion

☑ **Post-Launch (1-6 Months After Launch)**

- Gather customer feedback to improve products and services.
- Expand marketing efforts through strategic paid advertising.
- Develop partnerships with retailers and subscription box services.
- Introduce new product variations based on customer demand.

☑ **Long-Term Scaling Strategy** 🌱

- Explore additional revenue streams like bulk orders and corporate gifting.
- Build a community-driven loyalty program for repeat customers.
- Expand internationally through sustainable distribution channels.
- Continuously innovate products while maintaining the brand's eco-friendly mission.

This structured approach ensures a smooth launch while setting the business up for sustainable growth.

Made in the USA
Columbia, SC
30 June 2025

60171586R00093